TIME TO TURN AROUND

A LITERARY PROJECT BY THE INMATES OF
POTOMAC HIGHLANDS REGIONAL JAIL

FACULTY ADVISOR
Leslie Perry

PLEASE DIRECT INQUIRIES TO:
Breaking Barriers A Learning Center
38 Granite Avenue
Port Deposit, MD 21904

COVER ART
Frank Rose #3579683

DESIGN AND LAYOUT
Miranda Wilfong of Piccadilly Printing, Winchester Virginia

Time to Turn Around is privately funded.

TIME TO
TURN AROUND

A LITERARY PROJECT BY THE INMATES OF
POTOMAC HIGHLANDS REGIONAL JAIL

"DRIVERS LICENSE" — WILLOW LEZCANO

For my daughter—

You are the one who gave me the courage to travel my path, no matter where it took us. You encouraged me to embrace my purpose and to follow my dreams, even when others balked at my choices. You helped me to look in the mirror and believe in the person staring back at me. You picked me up off the floor when I was defeated and wanted to quit. You supported my career choice, although you were scared for my safety. You have always been in my corner. You have been my strength when I thought I could not keep going. Thank you!

I love you!

"THAT AIN'T YOU"

"Let me tell you something you already know. The world ain't all sunshine and rainbows. It's a very mean and nasty place and I don't care how tough you are it will beat you to your knees and keep you there permanently if you let it. You, me, or nobody is gonna hit as hard as life. But it ain't about how hard you hit. It's about how hard you can get hit and keep moving forward. How much you can take and keep moving forward. That's how winning is done! Now if you know what you're worth, then go out and get what you're worth. But you gotta be willing to take the hits, and not pointing fingers saying you ain't where you want to be because of him, or her, or anybody! Cowards do that and that ain't you! You're better than that!

— Sylvester Stallone, et al. ROCKY BALBOA. USA, 2006.

INTRODUCTION

I have worked as an Adult Education Instructor, specializing in GED, HiSET and TASC preparation for over 15 years. I started my career as a correctional educator in 2010 at the Pierce County Jail in Tacoma, Washington. At this regional jail I worked as the GEDplus Coordinator, assisting juveniles charged as adults, obtain high school credit and/or their GED.

When the pilot program ended, I relocated to Santa Fe, New Mexico where I worked as an ABE/GED Instructor at the Penitentiary of New Mexico, a maximum-security prison. Through spit shield doors, I helped inmates prepare for their GED exam. I also represented the education department at Re-Entry/ITap committee meetings, preparing education and transition plans for inmates pending release dates.

From New Mexico, I traveled to West Virginia where I worked at Potomac Highlands Regional Jail in Augusta, West Virginia. As the ABE/TASC Instructor, I prepared inmates to sit for their official TASC exam. In addition, students wrote resumes, letters of reconsideration, and took certification classes geared towards employment. This required many hours of homework. Yes, all my students were required to do homework, or they did not attend class.

The artwork, poems, and life reflections contained in this book were submitted by the inmates of Potomac Highlands Regional Jail in Augusta, West Virginia. This compilation started as a Project-Based Learning Assignment, a requirement to obtain my Career and Technical Education Endorsement at a graduate level. Project-Based Learning aids teachers in designing high-quality projects based on academic, as well as technical standards and is prompted by real-world scenarios. Project-Based Learning is a technique that allows students to apply what they have learned to real-life and see the finished product. You will find true, real-world scenarios in the poetry and reflections contained in this anthology.

This task was a real challenge because I worked in a jail and could not use teaching or class time to complete my project. It is my hope that the instructors who challenged me with this assignment, Dr. Brenda Tuckwiller, Dr. David M. Yost, and Associate Professor Richard Yocke will appreciate *Time to Turn Around.*

Being a part of this book was the inmate's choice. I did warn them from the beginning, that a simple first draft would not be enough. I instructed them that they would have many re-writes of their reflections and poems. Students who chose to participate checked out a thesaurus and dictionary to keep in their cell. Vocabulary and word choice became a wonderful teaching tool and inmates learned how to express what they wanted to say. Inmates who accepted this challenge made a real commitment to this project and set out to explain to their family, friends, and society how their choices put them where they are, and where they hoped to go in the future. For inmates, "future and hope" can be daunting words.

The inmates worked hard. Each entry was completed on their own, in their cells. None of the entries were class-time assignments. This is important to know because every single individual had an option to be involved in this creation. Frustrations came and went as their stories were returned from first draft editing. Crafting their feelings on paper and searching for words that expressed their true thoughts was seemingly impossible at times. Writing is hard for anyone, but some of these individuals had left school before the 9th grade and had no idea of just what they had signed up for. Sentence structure, grammar, punctuation, and spelling were the first hurdle. Once these had been corrected, they worked on what they were trying to say and the points that they wanted to get across to others. They shared their writing with other inmates for feedback and read them out loud to those in their pods to see if their stories made sense.

For weeks, even months, they worked. In the end, they found that they had a story to tell. They had a voice...their voice...a way to be heard. They were able to create and share their words and art without judgment knowing that one day, others would be able to read their stories and see where they came from. They learned to use their reflections and art to process their past actions, feelings, hopes, fears, and dreams. They found that they had an opportunity to tell their family, friends, children, and the world that no one needed to point a finger at them, they knew what they had done and what they had lost. Their hope is that others will make different choices.

I could go on and on. However, this is not about me. This is not my story. Through the years I'm sure that I learned more from the inmates I worked with than I probably ever gave back. This is my time to give back.

The following reflections and poems differ greatly, but each one tells a story. Not all inmates are incarcerated for crimes that would make your skin crawl. Over 80% of the inmates I worked with got lost in the system; drugs and alcohol were the instigators. As a society, we need to come together and look at the real problems. We need to treat the issues and find a path that leads to lowering recidivism. We need a plan, as a country, to address the barriers inmates face when they are released. We need to consider avenues we have not yet tried to implement and ensure opportunities for those who want a better life but believe they can't have one, or believe they don't deserve one.

As you read the following entries, take time to pause and reflect as one of these inmates could be your mother or father, your sister or brother, your best friend, your best friends' child. Incarceration is not just for the evildoer.

The individuals whose stories, poems, and artwork are presented in this book trusted me with their work. Every single one of them went the extra mile. Although this book took longer than I had hoped to publish, I am happy that I am able to see this come to print. I am eternally grateful for having the opportunity to work with this community.

Thank you,

Leslie Perry

ACKNOWLEDGEMENTS

Thank you to the professors at Marshall University, who pushed me to dig deep to develop *Time to Turn Around*, my Project-Based Learning Assignment. I am fortunate to have been given the opportunity to learn from Dr. Brenda Tuckwiller, Dr. David M. Yost, and Associate Professor Richard Yocke. These instructors provided me with the encouragement and "warm feedback" I needed to keep moving forward with the literary compilation.

My sincere gratitude goes out to the entire staff at Potomac Highlands Regional Jail. I want to recognize every part of this team; they all should be acknowledged. The support of my administrator, captain, officers, director of inmate services, medical staff, social workers, human resources, and maintenance crew enabled me to bring this project to fruition.

Special thanks to Kacey Corbett, who spent hours editing and proofreading. You inspired me to keep going. You are a truly amazing person. I am blessed to have you in my corner.

I am especially indebted to Piccadilly Printing and Miranda Wilfong. Their creative, personal, and professional approach for designing the publication layout for this compilation is greatly appreciated.

A grand salute also to the many others, who by their kind co-operation have assisted me in the preparation of this literary and artistic collection.

Leslie Perry

STUDENT ACKNOWLEDGEMENTS

First and foremost, we would like to give thanks and blessings to Ms. Perry for making this possible. She has a great heart and is willing to help anyone who wants to put forth the effort in helping themselves. She is every bit of the word amazing. Without her guidance, we would not have had the mindset to even be involved with this project. We appreciate everything she does.

During our time together, she has shown and taught us all that life can be what you make out of it—good or bad. In the end, it's all up to us. This project was about each and every one of us finding our own voice. To be heard one must find the courage to stand up and speak. She told us all, "Why not use what you have done, experienced, and realized to help others."

There are a lot of people involved in this project who had stories to tell that were never given the chance to do in the past. This made a big difference towards our perspective on life. Being involved in *Time to Turn Around* gave us all the opportunity to use our voices to be heard; to show our talents, and for others to see that sometimes people with good hearts make bad choices and get trapped in situations that are not always healthy. This was an opening for us to tell our stories in different forms and fashions—showing emotion—which most of us normally try not to do.

The purpose of making a mistake is to learn from it. We hope that everyone who picks this book up will try to understand that there are many people in the world who know when it is *Time to Turn Around*. This is our first step in making a change.

We would also like to thank each other and everyone who put forth the time and effort to be part of this project. Thank you!

The Students

TABLE OF CONTENTS

TABLE OF CONTENTS

PREFACE

Regular class periods were structured around the mechanics of writing, reading, comprehension and math. Sometimes however, I would show movies on a Free Friday. I chose movies to initiate a response, a debate, thoughtful reflection, and growth.

Students had the option to view the movie that was being shown. If they chose to watch the movie, I required a reflective essay that needed to be turned in the following Monday. These essays were not easy, and they had to be completed on their own time—over the weekend.

During the films, tempers often flared because content went against everything that they were taught or believed in. I would pause the movie at this point and encourage further discussion. Sometimes a student would opt to leave and not finish the film. Those that stayed had to turn in their best work. This meant proper spelling, grammar, sentences, paragraphs and answering the questions(s) to the best of their ability.

The following are some of the partial essays that were turned in for one of the Friday Movies, *"The Count of Monte Cristo."* Before the movie began, I explained what I was requiring them to reflect on while watching. I answered all questions the students had and what my expectations were.

They were given a handout before the movie started:

- *Write a reflective essay, two (2) pages in length.*
- *How is the main character, Edmond similar to you?*
- *How does Edmond use his situation to better himself?*
- *What is Edmond's downfall?*
- *What does Edmond learn from his suffering?*
- *If you really look, listen, and reflect on the movie, what did you learn?*

Alexandre Dumas asked more of his audience than one expects when they sit down to have a simple read or watch an entertaining film. I asked more from my students than they believed they could give and they succeeded.

I am thankful every day for the lessons my students taught me through their writing. They reminded me that we are more alike than different. And if you make a wrong decision, make a different choice. It is how we proceed that determines the outcome. For it is what we make of our situation that shows our true character.

STUDENT RESPONSES

"Edmond and I are alike in many ways. For starters, we were both betrayed by people we thought were our friends. Two people I considered brothers set me up by wearing wires. The only difference between Edmond and myself is that I committed the offenses that I'm locked up for.

I'm using my time incarcerated to better myself, as Edmond did in the film. I'm in class to further my education. I am also going to Narcotics Anonymous groups when they are available to help me with my drug addiction.

After being sentenced to prison, my significant other jumped ship and started dating one of my friends. Unlike Edmond though, I couldn't care less about that harlot. I'm no dummy by far. I knew, out of the gate, that she was only with me for the dope.

It is crazy though how everyone forgets about you when you go away. However, I don't plan on taking revenge like Edmond does in the movie. I am a firm believer in karma. I know that if they aren't here for me now, then they can forget about me when I am released. They obviously were not real friends to begin with.

I will get released one day and when I do, I will be a new person. My own version of "Monte Cristo" if you will. I will be a completely new person because of how I've used my time in prison, and that is what I'm really striving for."

ROBERT GABBERT #3538321

"Edmond is similar to me because we were both turned on by people that we thought were supposed to be "our" people. The people that he thought were his friends set him up and sent him to prison. In my situation, people that I thought were trying to help me and look out for me, set me up and sent me away to prison as well. I am now trying to better myself by going to class and trying to get every and all available certifications. I am also trying to stay out of trouble, even though sometimes it may seem like I am at my breaking point."

ISAAC MAUSALI

STUDENT RESPONSES

"I believe Edmond and I are similar in many ways. He is a natural leader and always tries to find the best in every person he meets. He has faith in God and doesn't give up hope…even in his unbearable surroundings. He is loyal to his family and friends and Mercedes. He loves adventure and does not back down from anything that comes in the way of what he believes in.

This story taught me many things. Sometimes life is hard and unfair. Sometimes the people that are the closest to you are the ones who hurt you the most. Be careful who you trust and always be aware of what other peoples' intentions are. That even though things may not be the way you want them to be, do the best that you can to make the most out of every situation. Keep hope alive in your heart and never give up. Keep trying, no matter how dark it gets. Never give up. Like me, and Edmond, you never know what's around the next corner."

JACOB GRACIA

"I like that while Edmond is locked away, he uses his time to better himself. He learns how to read, do math and how to fight with a sword. During my time in prison I've always taken classes: welding, blueprint reading 1 & 2, Thinking for a Change, RSAT and more. I have always tried to make the best out of any situation I'm put in.

What I learned from the movie is that no matter what life throws my way I should stay positive and make the best out of it. I should never give up and that I am never too old to learn something new. Last, but not least, I am king of this moment."

JESSE LONG #3558069

"The main character is similar to me in many ways. He got locked up and was incarcerated at a young age and seemed to lose everything he possibly owned. From the movie I learned that nothing is forever and if you set your mind towards the things you want done and want to achieve in life it is very much possible. Just never give up and always follow your heart and dreams. Life is short and is what you make of it."

TERRY GRAHAM #3546509

STUDENT RESPONSES

"In the movie Edmond uses his hate and anger to drive him. Like when I used speed to stay awake, or dope to forget. Edmond uses his feelings to punish and hurt the people that have hurt him or did him wrong.

Like Edmond, I have used hate and anger to push me my whole life; for good and bad, but most of the time it never ended well. I can relate to him because I've had some of the same experiences. My own family either left me or turned their backs on me when I needed them the most.

I forgave my family for turning their backs on me when I was just a kid. Just as Edmond forgave his girl after he realized that she never gave up on him. I know that my family had their reasons back then, but once I got my shit together, they showed me that they have always been there. They wanted me to figure things out on my own, just as Edmund needed to do.

In my life I've been at the bottom and I've been on the top. It's made me realize that there is so much more in life to enjoy and experience than using drugs. Once I got clean and stayed clean, I looked at everything differently. I enjoy life and I never forget my past because it's made me who I am today. Even though I've lost everything twice and been in and out of prison for the last eight years, I wouldn't change a lot.

I started out like Fernand; mad, jealous and doing whatever it took to get what I wanted in life, whether it was wrong or right. Letting my anger control my life was my way, until I decided to change and get help. This is when I became like Edmond; locked up and forgotten about, not seeing any future in life. Until one day, I decided that I didn't want to spend the rest of my life in and out of prison.

When Edmond met the priest in his cell and they made a deal, "One's help for the other's," he took a negative situation and turned it into a positive when all else was lost. He met one person that changed his whole life and turned it around. I started turning my life around on my own. I realized that I wasn't just hurting myself, but everyone around me. I didn't want to be that guy. I wanted and still want people to say that they were wrong about me, that they didn't see that coming.

I have taken time while being locked up to do everything in my power to gain something from serving time. I've worked on myself as a person. I've learned new trades in the work force and furthered my education, as much as I can.

I am never going to stop pushing forward. But I will always keep my past in mind. I never want to go back to my past lifestyle."

ERIC S. KNIBIEHLY II

STUDENT RESPONSES

"Watching, *The Count of Monte Cristo* was a real treat. Even better, hearing you say that I mainly had to personalize some similarity between Edmond and myself. Well, in my mind's eye that was a piece of cake!

Uneducated, I have kept myself trapped in this constant loop of insanity. Angry because of my loneliness and hating myself because of my fears. Oppressing myself has become the only way I know. Everyone says that your focus determines your reality. My reality is absolutely a living Hell, tormenting me daily to the brink of suicide. I've called upon God many, many times. Cursed Him, even changed religions. But still, no help came with my afflictions. But one day, like Edmond, "God shall set me free."

I believe Edmond's downfall was his lack of education and simply trust. He trusted without good sense which led to betrayal. A betrayal that nearly led to Edmond's demise.

Pain takes many days, sometimes years to pass. So, I will say that Dantes learned that there is no such thing as instant gratification when it comes to pain and suffering. I will also add that many years after you have achieved stability the mere thought of old love, long forgotten, can cut deeper than the original wound.

The world still consists of half-wits, jealousy, ambivalence, greed, love, tricks, and ambition. I've come to the conclusion that because of my uneducated ways I've been the maker of my own destruction.

Unlike Dantes, I deserve to be where I am today. This is why I am in class and giving it my all. I have tried everything else, except educating myself. Thank you for giving me a chance at success."

MICHEAL SMITH-BARROW #3350378

> "Anger is an acid that can do more harm to the vessel
> in which it is stored than anything on which it is poured."
> — *Mark Twain*

KING OF THE MOMENT

I'm king of the moment,
Oh yes, Lord of the day!
See, the victor's prize
In my eyes, here to stay.

So, I'm holding it closely,
All was given to you.
You put me in prison
Because you wanted mine too!

I thought we were friends,
Like brothers should be.
You lied and took my life,
Just to have the victory.

Now you've lost everything
And the tables have turned.
I'm king of the moment
Champions place I have earned.

*"When faced with a challenge,
look for a way, not a way out"*
— David Weatherford

SUBMISSIONS

TATTOOS

Some Prefer art in the form of pictures within
    A frame nailed on the walls. But 4 some,
    They Prefer their art in the form of ink, in the
Skin, So People can See, what they Can't See within.
    Every Tattoo Contains A story or A meaning.
It's a symbolization of one's Beliefs, or Memories.
    They're An Art, worn from Pain, 4 others 2 see.
Whatever the Reason may be, behind the ink, lies A Visual
    understanding of the individuals Personality, or Character.
All Pieced Together, 2 Modify the look of Blank Skin.

> "Show me a man with a tattoo
> and I'll show you a man with an interesting past."
> — *Jack London*

LOVE LOST

There is a Place that holds every Person's Love Lost.
That Place is stored with Pain, Hatred, and Anger.
Emotions that stem from Love, Branch into Hate & Unforgiveness.
The Truth is lying at the feet of wickedness.
An Abyss, where existing Love Turns into A fog at Hell's Gates.
Cold it is, with No Road 2 be found Again.
Love Lost, is Lost 4 ever.

> "Always forgive your enemies; nothing
> annoys them so much."
> — *Oscar Wilde*

JULIAN

From butterflies and bumblebees,
To smiling flowers on a summer breeze.
Songs of laughter through rays of sunshine,
All melodies of happiness, to brighten your mind.
You're an angel of beauty, and a rainbow of life,
When my world gets dark, you're a beacon of light.
So, when times get hard, and life gets you down,
Remember to smile, son, turn your frown upside down.

> "There is only one happiness in this life,
> to love and be loved."
> — George Sand

LYDIA

The soul of my heart, the love of my pain,
My scar that bleeds, forever in vain.
The night of my dreams, the good to my evil,
A beautiful nightmare, love with no equal.
The red of your lips, the rose to my thorns,
A crimson kiss, between halo and horns.
A shiver of touch, the chill on our skin,
From lust, to love, your breath I breathe in.
A taste of pleasure, between poison and sin,
I drink every drop, from beginning to end.
A whisper of screams, blinded by moans,
With my lips to your ear, I'm finally at home.

> "Happiness is the man who ventures boldly
> to defend what he holds dear."
> — Ovid

"BATTLE BORN 1" — ALLEN E. PARKER JR. #3479874   29

ISOLATION STATION

Confined inside this box with locks,
The steel doors and concrete floors,
Tempered glass, skew memories past,
Angry, I wonder how long I'll last.

No escape from this place I face,
Slowly killing time of mine, once more.
Everything I called home is gone,
Now, all alone, from dusk 'till dawn.

Happy thoughts transformed to gloom again,
I wake up every day to real pain.
No more freedom, just isolation,
Detached from the world in this station.

I try and attempt not to lose my mind,
Searching within until good I can find.
Time away can change a man for sure,
Turn around, be strong, and endure.

*"Every next level of your life will
demand a different you."
— Anonymous*

BETTER DAYS

Staring out the window, **HYPNOTIZED**, concentrating on rain drops.
Focusing on **BETTER DAYS** keeps me stuck in the **SAME SPOT**.
ACKNOWLEDGING my failures, pushes me forward, **IMPROVING** myself.
Lost in a train of **THOUGHTS**, I don't recognize the rain has stopped.

It hurts to say, "When I **CRY** it pours, like the sun does not **SHINE**."
Over time the **WETNESS** from the rain dries up.
The dew in the morning is **IMPOSSIBLE** to recognize.
TEARS on my cheeks flow from both my eyes.

DAZED by my past mistakes, I **REMINISCE** about **BETTER** days.
I try to learn from my wrongdoing, but it's **HARD** to stay straight.
Focusing on what's **RIGHT**, I realize, it's **ME**, I must blame.
I want the **BEST** for my life, **RIGHTFULLY** I need to change.

Staring out the window, **HYPNOTIZED**, concentrating on rain drops.
Focusing on **BETTER DAYS** keeps me stuck in the **SAME SPOT**.
ACKNOWLEDGING my failures, pushes me forward, **IMPROVING** myself.
Lost in a train of **THOUGHTS**, I don't recognize the rain has stopped.

"Lost time is never found again."
— Benjamin Franklin

Khaos

I TOOK MY OWN PATH

This is a brief look into my life; the road that brought me here has been rough. Things have been far from easy. There have been times when I felt like I had it all together and times where I felt like giving up. Somehow, here I am taking it day by day, the best I can and it's 2019.

I honestly can't tell you I had a bad childhood. I had parents who went above and beyond to make sure I had everything I needed. I started hanging out with older kids in school. I took my own path, as most do and that's where things went downhill. I started using drugs at 14, behind my parents back. My drug use began small, but of course that didn't last long.

Soon I was getting up early and running to my friend's house and not coming home until my mom called me late at night. My father passed away in 2011. His death hit my whole family hard. My entire world felt like it was coming down around me. I barely made it through high school. Somehow, by the grace of God, I graduated with my phlebotomy license and started at a community college. However, I ended up dropping out after only 2 months.

In 2013 things finally started to turn around for me in a positive way. I found out I was expecting my first born. I got clean and sober for the first time in five years. I applied to a technical school and received two certificates in nursing. 2013 turned out to be a year of accomplishments for me. I finally did something with my life. My son was a happy, healthy baby. Things went well for six to eight months; I was back working in home health trying to make ends meet.

As soon as the money was coming in my drug habit came right back. I fell right back onto the same path. Although I felt like I had everything under control, working and taking care of my kids; things slowly progressed. My second son was born in 2015. I had two happy, healthy boys who I loved more than life itself. Looking back now, I can't understand why they weren't enough to make me want to change my ways.

I thank God for my kid's father. Without him I have no idea where my boys would be now. By March 2017 things were 1000 times worse. I was working at Rubbermaid making damn good money. Steadily working, I chased my high. My drug of choice went from opioids to speeders. I couldn't hold a place to live; I was evicted from three different houses in a six-month period. I was in a vicious circle, constantly running around to either find or sell something to get a fix.

In October 2017 a friend introduced me to methamphetamine (meth). That was all she wrote. I've never had anything make me feel the way that drug did. By the end of 2017, I had lost everything that meant anything to me. My life was beyond unmanageable. In December, after a failed suicide attempt, I finally made the decision to try going to a rehab. I signed my children over to my aunt and went all the way to Bridgeport for my first try at rehab. I made it three days and got kicked out. I returned home and stayed clean for two weeks, but relapsed. My aunt, who had my boys, and everyone else in my life were fed up with my actions.

Without my boys, I went crazy. Drugs became my life. All I wanted to do was ride around and stay high. I didn't have a job and a friend of mine talked me into opening accounts and writing checks. I did it few times and realized it was a lot easier than other things I was doing to try to get high. So, I went around opening accounts. I found a website online where I could order checks and they would arrive in 2 days. My drug habit went crazy. I didn't care about the consequences I knew would come. I ended up getting arrested in March of 2018 for some of the bad checks I had written. I was in custody for 24 hours then released on bond.

Once again, I decided I was going to try to get clean. I moved away from my hometown and away from the people I used drugs with. It finally worked. I was clean for four months, but the checks followed me. I had been steadily writing them everywhere. Looking back now I have no idea what I was thinking, or how I thought any of it was okay.

In June 2018 I moved back to my hometown to try to make things work with my kid's father. He was allowed visitation with my kids and I thought since I was clean, I could move back and be with them. I was in town for three weeks when I began using again. Word got around that I had outstanding warrants and that the cops were looking for me. It wasn't long before a sheriff's deputy pulled up to the house with three warrants and two detainers. I knew then that everything I had been doing was catching up. I got arrested in front of my three-year-old son.

I've been incarcerated for almost nine months now. This is the longest I have been clean in 11 years except for the times I was pregnant. I haven't seen my boys in six months. When I call, they ask when I'm coming home? It absolutely breaks my heart that I can't tell them when that will be. I recently got sentenced to 1-10 years.

Jail has been an eye-opening situation. Before I was incarcerated it had been years since someone told me when to go to bed, when to eat, when I could go outside. I've missed out on so much with my kids. I've missed birthdays, their first day of school, and Christmas. I still have six months before I see if I'm eligible for parole. After that I have two other states to deal with before I'll be able to go home to my family.

I've had a lot of time to think about everything I have done. I regret a lot of my past decisions. Being away from my kids has made me want to do things differently when I get out. I would give almost anything to sit with my children and feel their arms around me. A year ago, I was running from them. I didn't realize what I had until I didn't have it anymore. I didn't realize at the time where my actions would lead me. A year ago, I would have never imagined bringing in 2019 behind bars.

I still have a long road ahead of me, but I'm optimistic for the future. I'm ready to be out with my kids and start my life over again. I want to be drug free and stable on my own. I want to be someone my kids and family are proud of. One day I'll be exactly where I want to be, but for now I take it one day at a time.

"Oh, my friend, it's not what they take away from you that counts-it's
what you do with what you have left."
—Hubert H. Humphrey

A FREEDOM THAT I NEVER HAD

I'm from a small town in West Virginia that you couldn't find on a map if you had a microscope. I was born in Annapolis, Maryland but was moved to Slanesville, West Virginia when I was adopted by two wonderful people. I was 3 months old.

My birth mother, Angel, is many great things: smart, loyal and intuitive. Despite all her wonderful qualities, she's an addict and has been since she was young. She didn't believe she could raise me properly, so she gave me to the best people she knew, hoping that I wouldn't go down the same path as her.

I'm thankful that I grew up the way I did. Although we didn't have all the money in the world, I never wondered if I was loved, or worried about my next meal. My parents taught me to always say, "Please and thank you." They told me to respect everyone, appreciate what you have and work hard for the things you want in life. They fought hard to shelter me from the things Angel had been exposed to growing up. I wasn't exposed to drugs. They raised me right. I eventually chose to do wrong on my own.

My adoptive mother passed away when I was 12 years old. This is when everything in my life changed. My dad, her husband of 36 years, fell into a deep depression. My dad is the best man I've ever known. He was devastated when he lost the love of his life. With my dad lost in his grief, I suddenly had a freedom that I'd never had.

Death is a hard process at any age, but at 12 it confused me. I was able to hang out with friends and my sister who turned out to be a terrible influence on me. Instead of grieving, I turned to partying. My sister, who was supposed to look after me, did the only thing she knew how to do. She started smoking weed with me and bought me alcohol. My sister quickly became my best friend and role model.

I spent my whole summer before high school hanging out with her; my new best friend and the 16-year-old boys that we liked. I started high school with a relaxed mindset about drugs and partying. I spent my first two years of high school getting black out drunk on the weekends and barely coming home throughout the week. Somehow, I maintained good grades, so it wasn't obvious to me that there was a problem developing. Yet I spent every weekend drinking and smoking, until I passed out. I experimented with other things, but nothing really interested me until I tried opiates at 17.

My sister, the only female role I had in my life at the time gave me my first Percocet 30. She had been the person who everyone counted on to protect me. My opiate addiction was gradual. I didn't hit rock bottom overnight. I hid it from my friends, my coworkers and my teachers. I got promoted to manager at my job and I went on to college where I did well for a couple semesters. My boyfriend and I both bought cars and rented our own place close to campus. On the outside it looked like I was kicking ass. At this time, my addiction hadn't taken over everything in my life. I didn't use every day. I would trade off between opiates and amphetamines, depending on how much I had to accomplish that day. I didn't feel any effects of physical dependency, so I convinced myself that I was doing good. I thought I was okay until my whole world flipped upside down. In a matter of weeks, I broke up with my boyfriend of four years, lost my apartment and quit going to school. The only stable thing that remained in my life was my job and even my work ethic began to decline.

In the middle of my life falling apart I looked for a place to stay. I knew a friend from high school who had just bought a house, so I moved in with him. I had no intention of having a relationship with him however we both loved to party, and without much thought we became intimate based off our mutual love for drugs. We spent the summer doing drugs that I had told myself I would never touch.

I enrolled back into classes for the fall semester, even though I was using. I didn't have a job, my boyfriend supported me and my habit. I convinced myself I was doing well. Somehow, I made it through the semester following the same pattern of alternating between substances to get through the term. Only now, I wasn't using Adderall, it was methamphetamine. It wasn't 30 mg of Percocet, it was 60. And when I couldn't afford the luxury of a $80 buzz, I settled for Suboxone.

My addiction gradually progressed to harder substances and much higher doses. I'm not blaming other people for my addiction. I know I made my own decisions. I take full responsibility for my drug use. I let those around me influence my behavior. My infatuation with my boyfriend and my lowered inhibitions, made me vulnerable and open to trying anything he brought home from work that day. Despite my love for opiates, I promised myself I would never touch heroin, but then my boyfriend of four years "graduated" to heroin.

After years of thinking I would never stoop to the level of doing the world's most hated drug, I decided to try it. I never understood it when people would say, "It only takes one time to get addicted." After using one time I caught myself thinking about it for days afterwards. I told myself it was a one-time thing. I can still remember having dreams about it throughout the week, after one night of trying it. Naturally I did what any addict would do, and I bought more. One bag led to two more, three more and so on. I kept telling myself, "I'm fine. It's just like any other drug that I binge on for a week at a time and put down for two."

Not long after my initial use, my life started to become unmanageable. I'd go into town to run a few errands and every place I'd stop I would go into the bathroom and take a couple hits. I justified it by telling myself, "At least I'm not shooting up in here." At the time I was working as a delivery driver at Dominos. On every delivery, I was taking back roads, stopping to "get gas" just to take a couple hits in the bathroom before I returned to work. Once the inevitable withdraws started happening, I quit my job because it interfered with my addiction. I was taking trips to Baltimore to get more product for a cheaper price, but it seemed as though no matter how much I got, I was out in the same amount of time.

Over the course of the next 10 months I became a walking zombie. I'm 5-foot-tall and never weighed over 100 pounds. At this point I was barely 85 pounds. I had no desire to do my hair or my makeup. The only time I left the house was to go buy cigarettes or take trips to the city. I was living a life that wasn't worth living anymore and I had no desire to change anything. I isolated myself from all the people that truly cared about me and pushed my boyfriend away. I was in a relationship with heroin, making it my number one priority in life. I surrounded myself with people that had no ambition, no goals, no jobs, nothing.

A lot of things that happened to me during that time period are a blur. I was hardly conscious. I don't remember much, but I do recall one memory vividly—I was laying on my bathroom floor one day, sick as fuck. I remember smoking a cigarette, freezing on a hot September day and I was crying. My life had become unmanageable. I wondered if I'd ever get away from the hold heroin had on my soul. I've never been a religious person, but in that moment I prayed. I asked whoever is out there looking over me in the vast universe to please help me fight these demons. I know you must have the desire to stop using and you have to change things in your life, but I swear after that day, there was a shift in my world.

Throughout the next couple weeks, I moved out of my boyfriend's house and started staying with a friend. Even though my friend and I were getting high together, our relationship was way more than that. I felt a connection to him that I hadn't felt in so long because my world had become all about drugs. He built me up. He reminded me of my potential every day. Yes, we were both using but he has never been like the other people I had met through my association with drugs. He's intelligent, he's kind, and he's genuine. We talked about the world, our lives before we knew each other, the goals we have, places we want to go. We spent many nights chilling under the stars, sharing secrets and falling in love. He helped me in ways I could never explain. It's the first time in my life that someone has never judged me or my past and has made me feel loved unconditionally. For the first time in a long time I cared about something other than getting high. I wish the happiness we felt together was enough to stop us from getting high but if you know anything about addiction, you know it's not that easy.

The only good thing I can say about myself is that I remained faithful to the morals I was brought up with. I never stole from anyone. I continue to put my trust in people and give them the benefit of the doubt. I am moving forward. I am on a journey to change.

> *"The pessimist complains about the wind; the optimist expects it to change; the realist adjusts the sails."*
> *— William Arthur Ward*

INTO THE SKY

Looking into heaven, **PRAYING** to God.
I ask, "Is it just me or are **YOU** taking your time?"
I know I have made **MISTAKES** which tore us apart, but,
You know me **BEST**, so why did you let me take it this far?

Staring into the sky, I **WISH** I could fly.
This world is full of **SINNERS**, I'm just trying to get by.
Losing **HOPE**, being somewhere the poor cannot survive.
Let the truth be known, **NO ONE** is ready to die.

Day dreaming, on my **KNEES**, I gaze up to Heaven.
Me heart overflows with aches, my **PRIDE** forbids surrender.
Currently I pay for Satan's **TEMPTATION**, does darkness call?
If I could change my past **FAILURES**, would I have a **FUTURE** at all?

Looking into heaven, **PRAYING** to God.
I ask, "Is it just me or are **YOU** taking your time?"
I know I have made **MISTAKES** which tore us apart, but,
You know me **BEST**, so why did you let me take it this far?

> *"Even though we can't have all we want, we ought to be thankful that we didn't get all we deserve."*
> — *Anonymous*

BLEEDING HEART

My heart bleeds red,
My soul, dying, aches.
I wish for freedom,
Outside of these gates.
I wear many a mask,
All reflect upon my past.
I've wasted many years it seems,
Now I'm lost, what does this mean?
ANGER TOWARDS MYSELF, OTHERS, AND GOD!
I do not deserve to live like this,
There's so much I'm going to miss.
I pray for strength and for wisdom,
Hoping, that God will finally listen.
All this loneliness is driving me crazy,
I'd give anything to smell or touch a daisy.
To count the stars, or feel the wind roar,
To listen to an airplane, as it soars.
I wish I may, I wish I might,
Know that next time, I'll do everything right.

> *"I will breathe. I will think of solution. I will not let my worry control me. I will simply breathe, and it will be okay because I don't quit."*
> *— Herman Hess*

HE'S TOO LITTLE TO UNDERSTAND

One morning changed my world entirely. Everything I loved in life, that I'd struggled to hang onto was placed in jeopardy. The past, which I hated, came back to haunt me. It's the day I learned what family really meant. It's when I learned what true consequences are; who is willing to hurt me, and who is willing to hurt with me. It's the day I came back to jail. The nightmare and heartache I never wanted again, came back.

I have been in trouble with the law. The first time I got caught, I was handed three "distribution" charges. I lost everything: my job, my home, my sons. The law took it all. I spent two years flat in jail. All I had to look forward to was a bag of coffee and two phone calls a week.

When I got out of jail, I vowed I would lead a better life and I'd never live in a cell again. For a while I succeeded. I got a job and a home. I met the man of my dreams and had my third, beautiful baby boy. I couldn't have been happier. The only thing that would have made my life perfect was to go back to court and gain custody of my twin sons.

My family wasn't close, and we didn't stay connected to one another. So, the day my cousin showed up at my house, I was excited. However, the first thing he did was ask me for a favor. He wanted me to lend him money, so he could start hustling. I tried to talk him out of it. I told him he didn't have to sell drugs to make money. I tried to tell him that he was smarter and better than that. I even talked to him about going back to school and getting a job. Nothing worked. I gave in and I gave him the money, because family is family.

After he got his drugs, he came back to my house. Shortly after he got there, the cops rolled up and caught him with the drugs. Since he was in my home when he got busted, I was charged with "conspiracy." In just a flash my whole world turned upside down. Back in cuffs and back in a jail cell. My nightmare returned; the heartache came back.

My cousin didn't care one bit that his mess destroyed everything I had worked so hard to put back together. I had been so proud of myself and my success. With these new charges. I was sentenced to a one to five in the state penitentiary.

My perfect man, the love of my life, and my son are now suffering on the outside without me. I sit here, back in jail, craving that one bag of coffee and two phone calls a week. Every day, I pray that I can hold on to the things I love so dearly. I believe my heart will not survive losing everything a second time.

Every time I talk to my son, I can hear in his voice how much he misses me. He's too little to understand why I am not there for him. It breaks my heart. I can't even imagine how my older twins feel. I'm sure they wonder why I haven't been able to come home to them yet. I was so close, but I let them down, again.

That day is going to haunt me and my family for a lifetime. Every hour I wish I could take that day, that hour, that choice, back. The moment I broke down, gave in, and handed my cousin that money; I let myself and my family down. I never wanted to sit in this position again. Yet, here I am—my stomach turning, and my heart torn apart.

I hope I will still be able to have a normal life when I return home to my family. I want more than anything to turn my life around. I want to go back to school and have a career. I am going to strive to move forward, like I was trying to do the day this all happened.

"You want to know the difference between a master
and the beginner? The master has failed more times
than the beginner has ever tried."
— *Stephen McCranie*

BEAUTIFUL

Attractiveness equals **FASCINATION**, resplendent means brilliant.
Magnificent is **MINE**, but mistakes are still present.
Strikingly gorgeous, was my **LIFE** in the making.
Focusing on the importance made my **ENTITY** amazing.

Mrs. America she is…**EVERYTHING** I ever wanted.
Forever's **PURPOSE** shows, our **LOVE** toward one another.
Waking up to **HER** brightens the existence we **SHARE**.
Lovely **TURNS** marvelous when she mentions having kids.

Picturing the sunrise, holding hands and running **INTO** the sunset.
Her **HEART** compares to loveliness. I will not **GIVE UP** for anything.
Forever **IS** eternal, "**I LOVE YOU**," with no **COMPUNCTION**.
Giving up is **NOT** in my thesaurus; I'm all yours with abundance.

Being all for her is a **BLESSING** to a charming situation.
Accepting **LIFE** as it's **GIVEN**, I live with love, plus forgiveness.
The wickedness, I have executed, placed me **BEHIND** correctional walls.
I now believe the **LESSON** of understanding, by which my **CREATOR CALLS**.

"Never to suffer would never to have been blessed."
— Edgar Allan Poe

THIS IS MY PRISON

This is my prison, made just for me,
Cold isolation, I can hardly breathe.
Darkness, seclusion, desperate defeat,
All freedom taken; loneliness peaked.

In my demise, all my cries go unheard.
No one will listen, to a single word.
Everywhere that I go, someone is there.
Any need that I have, nobody cares.

Why did this happen, when will it end?
I am so lonely and have not one friend.
What can I do to get out of this place?
If I could go back, my crime I'd erase.

There's no escaping this prison for me,
It's just my everyday walk, my reality.
I can't turn around, so I'll just move on through,
Stuck in this prison, with my sad rendezvous.

"There is hope, even when your brain tells you there isn't."
— John Green

PRAY 4 ME

There's A Battle within that's Being fought And No one Can See it.
The voice inside says, "There is Good in doing Bad Things." Am I wrong 2 See
Good in Bad Things? Am I wrong to see light in Dark Places?
Sometimes I look at Life But see nothing More than Regret.
Things that should Be Done Differently Become A Memory.
At Times when I think of Tomorrow, I think of God.
That's when Death Becomes Real.
But As Time Passes me by, I Become lost,
Just As fast as the very Thought was Discovered.
So, with No Particular Destination in Sight, with Days 2 Come
And the Path 2 Nowhere, Pray 4 me.

N
E
S
W

STRONGER

Where, underneath the stars,
Did ever we solve strengths?
Surely those who raise the bar,
Determine the weakest lengths.

Hard destructive pounding.
Through storms that crush and break.
We make our lives astounding,
Because of what we take.

Time makes all the difference,
Endure or fall apart.
Conquer through persistence:
Courage, strength, and heart.

Darkness never overcomes,
Bright and shining light.
Just remember we're the ones,
Who aren't afraid to fight!

"You never know how strong you are
until being strong is the only choice you have."
— Bob Marley

MY PERFECT RECIPE FOR MISERY

A broken heart is one of the most painful things I've ever experienced. There's an ache and sadness burning so deep within me; the only comparison I can make is burying a loved one. My broken heart was first, then I lost my home, my car, my job, **and** communication with my two-year-old son, who I was the primary care giver for since he came home from the hospital. This was my perfect recipe for misery.

Once I felt like I'd lost everything, it was easy to stop caring about anything. Standing on the precipice of despair my options were to either take a dive into the abyss or keep clawing and struggling to hold on to the seemingly hopeless, miserable, strands of life I had left. It seemed easier to just let go.

So that's just what I did. I dove into the nothingness, plunged into the darkness without looking back. Drugs and crime consumed my life; I fell into full throttle self-destruction. I felt it was either this or death and quite honestly, I would have chosen the latter, had my mother and sisters not just buried my father. No matter how bad I wanted to pull the trigger, the expressions on my family's faces, standing over my father's casket, always stopped me.

Drugs became my outlet; an overdose was inevitable, albeit not intentional. I continued to push the envelope on anything and everything around me. Thus, my downward spiral commenced. I began stealing cars and writing bad checks. I did this half in part to support my drug habit and half for the thrill and money. There was absolutely no discretion in my crimes because I didn't care if I got caught. I was wide open and wasn't stopping until I was dead or locked up.

In a twist of irony, everything came to a screeching halt one night in the middle of January 2017. I was speeding down a back road going over 60 miles per hour. I lost control of the vehicle I was driving, and wrapped the car around a beautiful oak tree and immediately lost consciousness. When I woke, I was at Ruby Memorial Hospital, had serious injuries, and several legal charges. Not long after, I found myself behind bars serving a two-year sentence in prison.

Since then, I have been trying to use my time to better myself and further my education. I have received my High School Equivalency and have completed several certificate programs. I plan to continue my education during the remainder of my sentence in prison. Upon my release, I hope to pursue a career in counseling or nursing. I want to work to get back and be the father that my son deserves and that I know I can be.

"Your future depends on many things, but mostly on you."
— Frank Tygen

VINCENT KELLY-ZITO #3414034 55

WALK AWAY FROM THE DRUGS

I sit at the tombstone in my cell, which is a table for anyone who is not an inmate. I think back over the years and replay the events that lead me here, to this point in my life. I doubt there are many people in society who'd understand the road to the cell. They don't see the pain, the abuse, or the loss I've dealt with in my life. No one knows how hard I've tried to overcome all the things that have broken me; they don't see how much I hate the person I've allowed those things to make me. All people see when they look at me is a worthless junkie and a criminal. It's so easy to judge others, but think what you could learn from learning my story. Many people overlook this fact and will never get the opportunity to learn from my experiences.

When I turned twelve, my father passed away. My whole life changed. My mother lost herself in grief, which in turn, destroyed the safe and secure family life I had been raised in. I was introduced to drugs and drinking by a mother who was rarely home. When she was home, her body would be right there in plain sight, but inside my mother was gone. I began pushing my pain down deep inside so it wouldn't show. At night that was never enough to keep the pain hidden from myself, so I followed my mothers' example and turned to drinking and drugs to numb my pain. When I needed love and guidance from my mother, I got a case of beer and a gram of cocaine. When I looked for a mother to open up to, she was either at the bar or passed out. This was the life I learned to adapt to until I turned fifteen which is when my life got worse.

My mom perceived me as a threat. I didn't understand why back then, and to this day I still wonder. I longed for my mother to love me. I yearned for some form of attention. But even when I received good grades and basketball awards, I got cussed out, torn down with words, punched and thrown to the ground. I just wanted to be loved, so badly that it blinded me. I began to lose sight of all the right in the world. I turned to drugs even more than before.

I started getting into trouble. I began stealing to support my drug habit. It seemed like the more trouble I got into, the nicer my mom was to me. The more drugs I bought home and shared with her, the more love she showed to me and I didn't get hit or mentally beat down. I had no rules, no authority, and no guidance. That is, until my brother found out. When he learned that "our" mom got me hooked on drugs, I ended up losing my family for a while.

It didn't matter where I went. I had a drug addiction. I had no idea how to overcome it, and no one to turn to for help. Then I met a guy. He had been in and out of jail, but that didn't matter. I fell deeply in love with him and we had kids. I felt as though I had finally found the love and family I yearned for. This man said all the right things, made me feel safe, secure, and loved. I finally thought I could walk away from the drugs, yet when I tried to the man that I would have taken a bullet for, cheated on me and began physically and mentally hurting me. I ended up losing the man and the family I prayed so hard for. I was left broken. I was alone with two kids to raise. Then, my brother saved me, again.

I hadn't realized that my addiction had turned me into a different person. My brother opened my eyes. He showed me my truth. He helped me to realize that the path I was walking down wasn't the right one. He made sure I saw my mistakes, but in doing so, he also made sure I knew I was loved. He told me that I meant the world to him. He had taken my hand and lead me out of the darkness. Yet, just as soon as he saved me, my brother was diagnosed with stage four throat cancer. In just a little over a year I watched him slowly lose his life.

The day I lost him, I lost myself. No matter how much I tried to get my life back on track after that I couldn't. I went back to not feeling. I went back to drugs. I ended up stealing money to support my habit, which in turn has gotten me where I am today. I will strive for a better future for myself and my kids. I am trying to be a better me. I want to try daily to go on without succumbing to my addiction. Today I am sober. That is enough.

> *"Some of us think holding on makes us strong,*
> *but sometimes it is letting go."*
> — Herman Hesse

WHAT IS LOVE?

Curse love, the feeling is totally fake.
It's nothing but broken promises and mistakes.
I grasp that I can't have love, without hate.

I'm trying to show you that you can believe in me.
The question I have is, "What did you ever see in me?"
I'm in my head—way **TOO** deep.

My heart is mutilated and I'm drowning.
I'm going under, I'm being dragged down.
I fear this is far from over.

I thought you were the love of my life.
Instead, you were sharp, like the edge of a knife.
The man inside of me, you cut him deep.

I hurt like I've been emotionally and physically beat.
My emotions have been bruised and abused.
The question remains, "Why should I LOVE you?"

*"There is no love without forgiveness,
and there is no forgiveness without love."
— Bryant H. McGill*

BRICK CITY

B7, cell 7, that's where I stay, or should I say the cage where I lay. It's all the same, just a different name. Close my eyes, another day fades, over and over, like ocean waves.

Don't rock the boat, go with the flow, you'll know when it's time to go. Everyone has a name, but only numbers show. Where are you from and who do you know? It's time to let your true colors show. On second thought... keep it on the low.

Patience, discipline, and self-control go a long way. Learn some respect and watch what you say. There are eyes and ears everywhere, slick words can make you pay. In here, you are never alone. Trust no one, you might make it another day.

This town is a brick city inside razor sharp fences. In here, it's different. Mind your own business. For instance... what you think you saw, you really didn't see. Stay in your own lane. In this community, you have no immunity. Quick hands are key. Stand your ground, "Homie."

Your word is all you have in here, so keep it true. If you steal in here, there's no telling what they may do. You might have to fight for your food, too. Are you still with me? I bet your mind's probably blown. You come here yourself, you'll leave here alone.

If you find yourself in this brick city, remember, there's no pity. Do what you're told. Always watch your back and don't be too bold, young, or old. Find your groove, and don't get too settled, always be ready to move. Jail is what you make of it. What you give is what you get.

There is one huge difference between you and me, think about it realistically. I got caught. You did not. You see, anyone could find themselves in here. I hope that's clear. You could be locked up and I could be free. There is **always** room in **my** brick city.

"If you don't like the road you're walking, start paving another one."
— *Dolly Parton*

EVEN IF

Even if I Showed you How I felt,
you'd look at Me As if it were in the eyes of a Stranger.
From the outside looking in,
Is As Good As Looking into A house That's Empty.
Seeing Pieces of life Bound Together,
Forced 2 take whatever it Can Possibly Hold.
But, at Any moment if Pushed Past its Boundaries,
Love will Break Away, And Be Left in Pieces.
Even if I Told you my struggles, while weighing Problems
On 1 shoulder And the other Containing A world of Hurt;
would you Truly understand, or would My Breath Be wasted?
Even if I took my Very Last Breath 2 tell you I Loved you,
would you Hear my Words Being Spoken from the heart?
Or, would you Hear A Voice Speaking, Without A Meaning?
Even if I could Fix what's Been Broken, would you Allow it to end up Broken
Again? Chained 2 these walls is the Battle I'm fighting within.
Even if you were 2 fight this battle with me, Am I fighting this Battle 2 win?

> *"A true relationship is two unperfect people*
> *refusing to give up on each other."*
> *— Anonymous*

REFLECTION

It's **SENSELESS** how things happen, unexpectedly.
For good or bad, those that mattered were left **UNPROTECTED**.
Mistakes were made—I have **NEVER SECOND** guessed them.
Individuals I thought were forever, **VANISHED**, the moment I chanced it.

Usually, people do not **SEE** eye to eye.
A reward given, honoring the **BADGE**, based **UPON** lies.
Knowing the intention was to **KILL**, no one should have survived.
God gave me a **VOICE**, for my friend, who **DID NOT** make it out alive.

It's **IRRATIONAL** how things happened, accidentally.
I was mentally crushed, **WATCHING** you get **SLAUGHTERED** & **DISSECTED**.
If I could **REWIND TIME**, I would have, **NEVER** chanced it.
Existing behind these **WALLS**, will never even the score, **MY BROTHER**.

Mistakes do not have to end with **BLOOD SHED**.
I still have night terrors, the gun shots, which **TOOK** his last breath.
That moment I understood, "Life **IS** precious," I wasted **OUR** last chance.
SECONDS too late, he did not **ESCAPE** the fall of death.

This chapter in my life, I **REPLAY**, over and over.
The **DIFFERENCE** between my past and my present is that I'm **SOBER**.
Looking at the pictures, I examine our **FAMILIES** suffering.
If I knew **THEN**, what I know **NOW**, my friend's **LIFE** might not be over.

"Every saint has a past, and every sinner has a future."
— Oscar Wilde

TOO MUCH

Taste of bitter darkness,
Perfectly alone.
Learning to be heartless,
Hate, I've never known.

Trapped inside this prison,
Nothing can compare.
Hidden terrors risen,
Wretched and unfair.

Human life consumption,
How long has it been?
Wickedness, corruption,
Rotting me within.

Everyone has limits,
It's gotten out of hand.
Trapped inside with misfits,
At the edge I stand.

Every day that I've spent,
Dare, I make it through?
Paralyzed confinement,
In the darkness without you.

"KOI" — ALLEN E. PARKER JR. #3479874   65

SON,

Hey bud, it's Daddy. I'm sorry I'm not around. Please know that it's nothing that you did, it's what dad did. Tearing us apart and away from one another is a result of some of the bad things Daddy did. I regret my actions each and every day. I must live with the choices I've made. This truly makes me sick to my stomach.

The happiest I've ever been in my life is when the two of us were together. Ever since you were born, we were inseparable; 24/7 we were side by side. You were my little partner. It's funny now that I sit back and think about it, you had to make it a point to have everything I had. It's as if you looked up to me in some way. I'll let you in on a secret, "You are the one who was getting looked up to." You are stronger than I will ever be.

I know your too young to understand what happened and why it happened. One day, you will come to realize what the real story behind my situation is. When you do, I hope you can find it in your heart to forgive me so that we can pick up where we left off. You are in God's hands right now.

Grammy is going to make sure you are alright and well taken care of, just like she did for Daddy growing up. Listen to her and what she has to teach you. Pappy is close too, just a phone call away. Any time you feel scared or alone pick up Daddy's picture and look at it. Close your eyes and picture the two of us having the best time of our lives, cutting up and poking fun at each other. I promise that the darkness will leave and go away.

Life is going to seem unfair and tricky at times, don't let that stop you or get in the way of what you truly want to achieve and accomplish. This is when you will come to realize that nothing will be able to stop you or hold you back from what you truly want.

As you grow older reality will start to clear things up. I hope and pray that when it does you will not hold a grudge against me. I want you to learn and grow from my mistakes. Every time I look at you, I see myself. It's really amazing, but then again, this fact scares me to death. I pray that as you grow older you will not follow in your father's footsteps.

My whole life seemed meaningless and out of control. I did things for all the wrong reasons, that is until you came into my life. At the very moment you were born I realized what true happiness was and what it felt like.

Now that I am in the situation I am in; I catch myself daydreaming about the past and all the wonderful memories we've made together. I wonder if things could have been prevented, or stopped, before they became so out of hand. I truly understand that what I did was selfish and unfair to you in every way.

My son, please find it within you to forgive me. My nonsense haunts me every day. I must live with that. So, until the day we meet again I keep you safe in my heart. I love you more than you'll ever know buddy and I always will, no matter what may happen between us. From my heart to your heart… always gone, but not forgotten.

Please, please do not ever decide to become what and who your dad has become. If you put your mind, heart and soul into something else you can achieve and become so much more than me. Hugs and kisses son, with love.

Love and sadness,
Daddy

> *"If you don't leave the past in the past, it will destroy your future.*
> *Look what's in front of you, not what yesterday took away.*
> *The best is yet to come."*
> *— George Strait*

HIT BY AN I.E.D.

I am writing my reflection from my cell. I sit on the lower bunk in my cell while other inmates watch TV and play cards in the dayroom. I knew I wouldn't be disturbed while I wrote this because all the inmates in my POD are busy. I joined the United States Army right out of high school, and I was deployed four times. While enlisted, and during my last deployment, the motorcade I was in got hit by an Improvised Explosive Device (IED). My military career ended there.

I was medically discharged me from the Army because of the accident and my mental health. I had a lot of problems dealing with being out of the Army, so I went to get help. The doctors told me that I had Post Traumatic Stress Disorder (PTSD). I knew some of my friends had this, but I never imagined I would suffer from it, or how I would handle it. I didn't know what to do when the doctors told me I would need to be on medication for the rest of my life to manage PTSD. All throughout my military career I was told that taking medication was a sign of weakness. So, instead of taking the prescribed drugs, I turned to using street drugs to deal with my PTSD.

The drugs quickly started to take over my life. They took time from my family and friends. Soon I began stealing from my loved ones to pay for my drug habit. I thought I would never get busted. I was wrong. In June of 2015 I got in to trouble for the first time in my life. Busted for drugs. I thought I would never get sent to prison because I had fought for my county and for everyone's freedom. I was wrong again. The courts ordered me to report to the West Virginia Division of Corrections. Mt. Olive Correctional Center is where I began my 1-10-year sentence.

Not long into my sentence I was transferred to St. Mary's Correctional Center. While incarcerated I was able to go to college. Then things changed. I went from attending college in a facility where I was not afraid, to being transferred to Huttonsville Correctional Center, where I became a little more frightened. In this facility people were doing a lot more time than me. I was housed in a cell with a guy that was in prison for killing five members of his family. I stayed in Hustonville Correctional Center until September 25, 2017. On this date, I was released from prison and placed on parole.

I had been serving a 1-10-year sentence but got released after 3 years. My life had changed dramatically during those three years. Some things were positive, but others resulted in loss. I've been told that time heals all wounds. In certain cases, I believe that might be true. Other times I believe this is false.

I made it out on parole for one year. However, I got picked up and re-arrested for not showing up to the parole office. Come to find out, they had sent my paperwork to the wrong state! I cannot believe I'm in prison again. I promised myself and my family that I would never go back to prison.

I look around me, just as the big metal gray door slams shut behind an inmate. I'm in a two-man cell just like last time. The cells are made for two, but they never just put two inmates in them. There is a tiny window to look out and see the outside world I cannot reach.

I hate this place! It stinks worse than the high school locker room after football practice. The air never moves. Staring at my state issued oranges, white socks, and sandals, I can't believe I am back in this place. I have two years left to go until I kill this one-to-ten. I am now 38 years old. I am a veteran of the United States Army. I served This country to the best of his ability. I am a veteran living with PTSD. Because of drugs, I live with a felony on my record.

"We cannot change anything unless we accept it."
— Carl Jung

DREAMS

Dream a dream and live your life,
Then live a dream come true.
Every success that you have,
Always depends on you.

Dare to dare and carry your cares,
Determine who you are.
Greater goals and possibilities,
Excel to take you far.

Hopes of lovely paradise,
Bring thoughts of ecstasy.
Take the road that leads you there,
Arrive...eventually.

Test your thoughts and rest your mind,
Believe in faith inside.
Tomorrow is a brand-new day,
You should never hide.

"Rise above the storm and you will find the sunshine."
— Mario Fernandez

Rose

THOUGHTS

Can't get rid of these thoughts in my head,
Instant playbacks of what people have said.
How do I make myself not care—become cold?
This life that I live has definitely become old.

I numb the pain that others cannot, because I can't change my weakest flaws.

It feels like everything has turned evil now.
Everyone around me is so hateful and foul.
My internal giver is downright broken.
All my kind words have been outwardly spoken.
I keep trying to harden my heart, every day.
This is the last time I will ever be treated this way.

"Growth and comfort do not coexist."
— Ginni Rometty

PLAYING KENO

The reason I ended up in jail is for violating my parole. In 2013 I was charged with embezzlement. These charges hurt me, my family and my relationship with my boyfriend. It has cost me time, money and jobs.

It all started because a co-worker and I got into playing Keno. We would run tickets, win, then pay our tab. After a while it got to where we didn't win, and we had a hard time paying our tab. This is when I started erasing my tab, so I didn't have to pay for my Keno. That is how I got caught and charged with embezzlement. This is also when I realized I had a problem gambling.

This didn't only affect my life, it affected everyone around me. I was a recovering addict and I started drinking heavily again. I began drinking around the clock. Sometimes I'd drink in the morning before work, then during work and after work. Soon, I started back using drugs, along with drinking. This put stress on my family, my relationship with my boyfriend and my job.

I was at a point that I didn't care if I went to jail. I didn't care about what anyone else thought. Everyone around me who cared said, "Misty, you need to slow down, you are rolling too fast. You are going to end up in jail." I blew everyone off, like I was invincible. I thought the embezzlement charges were really nothing. I believed I wasn't going to jail. Boy was I wrong! On all accounts.

I was charged in 2013 and indicted in 2015. I went to trial and took a misdemeanor charge instead of a felony. They suspended a year of jail time and gave me five years' probation. I should have done the jail time instead of probation.

Due to the death of my mother in 2016, depression and my charges, I became an alcoholic. I put my family through hell the last three years. This charge has fucked up my whole life. Now I sit incarcerated. I plan on going in to court and finishing out my sentence, which is another three and a half months. Hopefully, when I'm released, I can get my jobs back. Or, maybe, I'll find a better job so that I can get my life back on track.

I have missed out on holidays with my family, which I had never missed before in my life. I lost a relationship with my boyfriend of six years. I missed out on all the freedoms I had: driving my car, working, dirt bike riding with my kids, going camping with my brother, swimming with my nephew and many other things that I cannot do being in jail.

It has been a huge burden on my family having me in jail. They have to put money on my books so that I can call home. When I do call home from jail it makes me cry. The only thing that is good about me being in jail is that my family knows where I am at and they don't have to worry about me getting into trouble or going to jail; I'm already here.

So, if you have never been in jail, think about all the things you love and would miss if you are thinking about doing something illegal.

> *"A confession has to be part of your new life."*
> *— Ludwig Wittgenstein*

BLACK SHEEP

I've heard the term "black sheep" a million times since I turned 16. My whole life I've felt a little different than others. When I was young girls my age were going shopping, getting their nails done, and having their parents buy new cars for them. They had new cell phones. They could go out every weekend without having to beg and fight about it with their parents. I felt as though they suffered from "spoiled brat syndrome." On the other hand, I was at home cutting firewood, shoveling cow and pig shit, gathering eggs and mowing hay.

I never missed a basketball, volleyball, or softball practice. After practice I would go home and practice more, so I would be "good enough." I used to get mad at my parents and I never understood why they didn't let me go be crazy like my friends. I just wanted to fit in with the other people my age. I now know why my parents acted the way they did. They were trying to prevent me from sitting in orange like I am today, writing this.

The older I got, and the more I tried to fit in, the more drugs I began doing, until drugs were all I knew. I began sneaking out, lying, stealing, and getting into trouble. I didn't care and I didn't do anything quietly.

Thanks to all the sports I played I was well known in the town I'm from. My pap was the sheriff and my dad was the big boss of a major corporation. The pressure I felt to be great was intolerable and it was almost impossible to get away with anything without my family finding out. I ran my family's name through the mud. This was just the start of a downward spiral that lasted the next 9 years.

I can still remember when I was very young that I promised I would never do drugs when I grew up. Only bad people did drugs. Needless to say, I became one of those bad people doing drugs. My drug addiction began with smoking weed and drinking. That quickly escalated to pain pills and cocaine. I sit here today in orange, behind bars because I found heroin and a needle.

When I went to rehab for the first time, I did it for all the wrong reasons. I wanted to make everyone happy and help my mom feel better. I believed that I didn't have a drug problem, I was just having fun. At least that's what I told myself. I did my 28 days and came home. Within a week I was doing the same things that I'd done before. I preformed this dance for the next 2 years. I went to rehab, caught my breath, and stayed long enough for my tolerance to go down and my relationship with my parents to begin to heal. Then, I went home, fucked it all up, and lost everything, again and again.

My drug use has got in the way of my family, my friends, my sisters, and my job. I didn't care how bad things were, or who I was hurting. All that I cared about was my next high. I was so deep into my addiction that I forgot everything, my morals, values, where I came from, how I was raised and my family. I forgot what life was like before drugs. I forgot who I was. The only thing worse than losing myself, was not missing myself. That's what heroin did for me.

In the midst of my drug use I started catching charges. So, I said, "Fuck it!" It was all downhill after that. In May of 2013 I got indicted, because of my drug use. In October of 2013 I took a plea. At the age of 20 I became a convicted felon. I agreed to participate in the South Branch Valley Drug Court program.

I started attending classes, therapy, and did my community service. Immediately I knew I had made the biggest mistake of my life. Not because of the structure, or the educational classes, or the intense therapy sessions, but because they wouldn't let me get high. The only reason I agreed to do Drug Court, was so I didn't have to go to prison. The therapists, counselors, and other staff were hip to my "bullshit." After one of my many sanctions, the Drug Court director told me that I was being put up for termination. Termination meant that I would be kicked out of the program and sent to prison.

I wasn't ready for that, so I agreed to house arrest. I had to agree to house arrest at my mother's house. Drug Court made me go back to my roots. Somewhere amid getting up at 4:30 a.m. to bottle feed baby lambs, to programming from 8 a.m. till noon, then doing my community service until 4 p.m. I began to find myself. In finding myself, I began to love myself and realized I was lovable again.

I began excelling in drug court and actually WANTED to be clean and sober. My life was coming together through hard work and my desire to succeed. Then I met a guy who was also involved in Narcotics Anonymous. He lit up a room when he walked in and could make me smile instantly. We became inseparable. He was my best friend. I admired him too much and became co-dependent on him.

I stayed clean and worked my program. However, when I got off of house arrest, I began a relationship with Cruiz Cameron. I got pregnant and on July 16, 2015 we were blessed with our son, Ryker Bleu. I focused on being the best mom in the world, but I stopped attending meetings and reaching out. I quit doing the things I'd worked so hard to accomplish and started doing things that made me comfortable. I fell back into my old ways and did what "had been" familiar to me.

When Ryker was 3 months old, Cruiz and I started using again. At first it was fun, but then the vicious cycle became my reality once more. Slowly, but surely, I got strung out again. My heroin addiction picked up right where I left off and after a few months of chaos and disorder I decided to go back to rehab. This time it was my decision to go. After a few weeks of getting back on track with my sobriety I was finally starting to be happy again. Cruiz had also made the decision to go get clean. He went to a sober living house. On May 9, 2016, at 7:09 p.m., my mother contacted me at the rehab. Cruiz had lost his life and his battle to addiction. The day that Cruiz died, a part of me died with him.

Pain changes people. I'm proof of that. I know that there is something inside of me that's stronger than my pain. That inner something that helps me keep going in the face of adversity. I thought I was dealing with the death of Ryker's' father, but I was wrong. When I got home after rehab everything reminded me of him. I couldn't cope. I tried to distract myself by working all the time.

While working I met my youngest son's father, Brandon. Brandon and I started seeing each other. We did fun things together, but I was using him to fill the big, black hole in my heart. Brandon was a nice guy, but he was also a drug dealer. No surprise, I started using again. This time the consequences were much worse. I screwed up probation and every healthy relationship I had. Everything good in my life turned bad. To top it all off, I found out I was pregnant again. Bentley Grae was born July 20, 2017. Unfortunately, when

Bentley was born there were drugs in his system. I still can't forgive myself for this. On July 25, 2017 my probation was revoked, and I was sentenced to prison.

I got released from prison on April 9, 2018. I was so excited to go home and see my babies. I still remember the look on Ryker's face when he saw me. It was so precious. His eyes got so big and he smiled his little grin that melts my heart every time. I picked him up and he put his head down on my shoulder and hugged me. We stayed like that for over 5 minutes. Tears just ran down my face the whole time.

Little Bentley on the other hand, just looked at me. He didn't know who I was. I've never felt more like a piece of shit than I did then. Once I started talking, he recognized my voice and smiled. That moment I swore that I would never leave those precious faces again. I never wanted to go through that pain again. I would rather take a physical beating than be emotionally defeated like that. I did well for a few months. Slowly, but surely, I started hanging out with old friends again.

Eventually I started using again. I unleashed the monster I fought to contain. This time, my parents who have ALWAYS been there for me just didn't know what to do. I gave up. I believed my children were better off without me. I quit going to check in with my parole officer and ran. All my problems were the result of my drug use. I know drugs ruined my life and cost me everything. At the same time, drugs were the only thing that made me feel better.

Now I'm currently waiting to go back to prison. I've come to realize that I'm not a bad person trying to get good, I'm a sick person trying to get well. I'm not proud of some of the things I've done, but they have made me who I am today. I'm grateful for the little things. I know what it's like to have nothing.

Sometimes I'm my own worst enemy, but at the end of the day I have a family who loves me unconditionally. This is the most important thing to me. Most people would kill to have a family like mine. I still miss my children more than anything and would give anything to be with them, but this is the consequence of my actions. I make the days count, instead of counting the days.

May 8, 2016 was the last time I spoke to the love of my life and my best friend. Sometimes I sit and think or see something on the television that reminds me of Cruiz, and an overwhelming sadness comes over me. I'm an emotional drug user. As a matter of fact, drugs are the only way I know how to deal with my emotions. I know it's okay for me to cry and go to that dark place his death takes me. And it's ok to feel the raw that comes with it, but it's not okay for me to stay there. I know the good in me is most definitely stronger than any bad.

My parents are still the most influential people in my life, I don't know where I would be without them. I've learned that sometimes helping other people is the best help I can give myself. I'm not here to compete with anybody. I hope we all make it. I now try not to take things, or people for granted, because not everyone is promised tomorrow.

It is a combination of different things, little things, that most people overlook that are helping me to be humble today. I don't have bad days anymore. I have good days and learning days. I look at my past and those were bad days. Today I'm more fortunate and there is hope for tomorrow.

"I learned long ago that in order to heal my wounds,
I must have the courage to face up to them."
— Paulo Coelho

   ANONYMOUS

WHERE ARE MY PARENTS?

Everyone goes through some type of struggle in their life; some people just hide it better than others. I was born in East Cleveland, Ohio. I have four siblings: two older sisters, one older brother and one younger brother. We were split up between family members when we were young. My youngest brother and I lived with my paternal grandmother until I was almost 10 years old. She was my savior. My grandmother worried about her health and her own children; yet she always made sure my brother and I were taken care of.

Growing up I remember asking her, "Where are my parents?" My grandmother kept me in the dark about why my parents were not in the picture. It took me a long time to realize that my parents had lost custody of my brother and me.

My grandmother had told me stories about my mom. However, at the time that was not enough for me. I wanted to know what my mother looked like, who she was, where she was. As for my father? Eventually, he started writing to me from prison. He apologized for leaving us and told me that he would be getting out of prison and coming home by the time I turned 10.

My father didn't come home until I was 11. My brother and I both went to live with him, upon his release. It took a few months for us to adjust to the changes in our living arrangements, but slowly it all fell into place. We got comfortable. Most of the time it was just me, my brother and my father; although he did have girlfriends who came in and out of his life.

After a couple of years living with my father in a rundown area in Cleveland, things evened out. I often wondered how my dad supported us working the type of job he did. It soon occurred to me that he might be back doing the illegal things that got him placed in jail the first time. Of course, I never mentioned this to my father; I just stayed in a child's place. My dad always made sure we had the necessities, but most the time we didn't get things we wanted.

When I started the 8th grade my father began treating me more like a man, which I respected. I had to grow up at fast, and at a young age because he'd leave me at home to tend to my brother. I started running the streets. My father was never home to tell me what to do or not to do. I wanted the things my friends had: new shoes, name brand clothes, a nice smart phone, etc.

By the time I started high school I was running the streets, just like my father. I sold drugs and did things that I had no business doing. Since my father wasn't there half the time, I felt like it was up to me to support my little brother. I started skipping school because I couldn't make money while I sat in a classroom. My only motive was to sell drugs and that's exactly what I did. Until I got kicked out of school for bringing drugs onto the property.

This is when my father made me move to West Virginia to live with my maternal grandma and my sisters. I was devastated. I was moving to a new area, forced to leave my 13-year-old brother behind. West Virginia was a whole new world for me. I met my sisters for the first time in person after years of only talking to them on the phone. I hoped that by living with them I'd get an explanation as to where my mother was.

The first time I met my mom it brought tears to my eyes and I cried. I was happy to finally meet her, but it broke my heart to see her strung out on drugs. I was 17 years old. So, at 17 I didn't have a father figure around to guide me towards becoming a man. My sisters were like my best friends, and my grandma passed away due to congestive heart failure. I felt like I had no options, or hope. I went back to selling drugs. You would think I would've learned my lesson after being expelled a few years earlier, but I had an "I don't care" mentality. I went to school and got decent grades, and sold drugs.

Although it appeared that I was only worried about making money and having the latest things I decided to give my mother a chance to be a mom. I didn't have one growing up. She was around a lot right before my graduation from high school and even more once I did graduate. As our relationship began to strengthen, I watched as her body weakened. My freshman year of college she was diagnosed with stage 3 breast cancer. She passed away my sophomore year of college. I felt like I lost her, faster than I got her. It tore me up inside.

I thought things couldn't get any worse after losing my mother. I was wrong. I got a call one day informing me that my youngest brother had been shot and killed; back home in Cleveland. He was only 15 years old. I didn't think I could carry on with my life. He was my best friend. I felt like if I would have made better decisions, I would never had to leave him behind. Maybe I could have guided him down the right path. I knew that I needed to do something different with my life or I was going to end up in the same situation as him.

I applied to Fairmont State University and was accepted. I attended college from the fall of 2014 until the spring semester of 2016. Inside I felt that I deserved better and needed more of a challenge, so I transferred to

West Virginia University. At this point I was selling several types of drugs and felt unstoppable because of the things I was doing. Somehow, I still managed to get my schoolwork done.

I stayed this way until my girlfriend told me she was pregnant. At that moment I had to make a choice, attend school or get a legal job and focus on the baby that was coming soon. A lot of things are easier said than done. I was addicted to the fast life. I continued to go to school, but I was more worried about supporting my family. So, instead of chasing a degree I focused on the streets, knowing deep down that it wouldn't get my very far.

Soon after my baby was born my life went in another direction, not in a good way. I stopped showing up to class. I was tied to the wrong things, with the wrong people. People tried taking advantage of me, tried to rob me. I was so deeply involved in the streets that I didn't know how to put my pride aside. I sought revenge which ended up placing me in jail at 21.

I let the streets take control of me and looking back it wasn't worth it. I've been incarcerated for several years now. I let my daughter down and ruined my life at a young age. If I could go back, I would definitely do things a lot different. If I could give others advice, I would encourage all young adults not to take the same path as I did just because of your surroundings. Stand up and be yourself, it will get you a lot further in life and you will be satisfied with the results.

I once read a quote by Victor Hugo which I try to live by now, "Never dwell on your mistakes just remember them and learn from them."

Although my life has been put on hold, I still am making the best of it any way I can. I am a strong person. I will succeed, no matter what roadblocks come my way.

> *"Let today be the day you give up who you've been*
> *for who you can become."*
> *— Hal Elrod*

BY ANY MEANS NECESSARY

I have witnessed a lot on the streets. I'm only 27 and I have made a lot of mistakes. My mom was alone, raising my four brothers, five sisters and myself. I had to adjust to the life that I was living. My father was never around.

Growing up, my mother had to teach five boys how to become men, by any means necessary. She did just that. My mom was sick. I remember worrying. Just about the time I realized what was killing her...cancer...things got worse.

My oldest brother Christopher was paralyzed from the waist down. Then my oldest sister, Christina was diagnosed with cancer behind her eye and she had to start radiation treatment. Soon after, my little sister Christal, was diagnosed with Sickle Cell Anemia. The doctor told my mother that my sister wouldn't make it past her sixth birthday. My little brother Chrisjamar was having Grand Mal Seizures and the doctors prescribed a steroid treatment to help support his heart. All of this made my mother very depressed.

While all of this was happening my mother was slowly dying from cancer. I made a vow to be nothing like my father. Instead of taking care of his family, he was looking for drugs to support his addiction. He was somewhere looking to find his next fix.

Our family was breaking down. By the age of 13, I had become a man. The streets were never my choice to turn to as a child. In fact, as a kid, I always had dreams of wanting to become a police officer. But, in trying to help support my family throughout our struggles I got in to trouble. The trouble I got in to took away my childish dreams.

Over the next few years, I became cold hearted. Because I had such a hard life as a child, I began to feel less and less. Because I had not been able to do the things that I wanted to do as a little boy I started to hate others, blame others. It's sad to say, I had become a problem child.

School was supposed to be a place where I could learn how to be anything I wanted to be. Instead, by the 11th grade I found myself getting expelled from school for bringing drugs on campus. Night school is what the school board recommended, but I chose the alternate—home school.

Sports gave me an outlet. I found them helpful and I loved to play and compete. Football, basketball, art and choirs were like my safe heaven. These places made me feel like I did have a purpose in life. In the 12th grade, I started attending South Charleston High School; George Washington High School didn't want me on their campus anymore. Switching schools took the breath from my heart. I was not allowed to join any sport clubs at the new school. In order to have been eligible to play sports I had to be at that school for at least one year. So, without sports I focused on my grades and managed to graduate on time with my class in 2011.

In November of 2017, age 25, I made my biggest mistake. I found myself charged with attempted 1st degree robbery, burglary, and murder. I was facing life behind bars. On October 12, 2018 I pled out to attempted 1st degree robbery without the use of a firearm, in return they sentenced me to 10 years flat.

This time away has and will always be a reflection on my life. What I've been through in life has been a learning opportunity for me in many ways. It has taught me that life comes with a purpose, and at times you will make mistakes.

I know now that it's learning from you mistakes that counts. Understanding that life can only be lived once, so everyone, including me needs to make best out of it. I am looking forward...this is my Time to Turn Around.

"Where there is no struggle, there is no strength."
— Oprah Winfrey

ALL THIS TIME

All this time, where did it go? And for this, what's there to show?
I have memories which get me low. Terrible dreams, wouldn't you know?

The lessons I've learned, and two years served, was rough.
Can I use these lessons to help other souls, do I care enough?

All this time, I do believe, has taught me something…definitely.
There is no one to blame but myself, I am my worst enemy.

What is next, in this thing called life and just how will it end?
All this time I've spent, should keep me from coming back again.

Will I help others? Save them from this from fate? I will try my best.
Will they heed my advice, or dance the dance and fail the same test?

All I can do is hope and pray. Maybe I'll save someone, one day.
Until that time, hear me, take my advice, and listen to what I say.

Always do the best you can, in everything, and never give up hope.
Love yourself, enough to work hard, be brave, don't get down with dope.

"I've seen my fall. I shall, one day, witness my rise too."
— KM

CEMENT

Surrounded by white walls and cement
Reflecting on what everything truly meant.
Nothing's worth this lonely feeling, I lied.
It's been a long time since I've sincerely cried.
Starting to become numb inside,
Letting go of guilt, winning back my pride.
Life is a lesson I try to reflect upon,
I feel better, with each waking dawn.
Sometimes we never know why, or when,
But all that matters, is we're okay within.
As long as I do right every single day,
I wake up, breathe out, and I'm okay.
If I take no steps back, move only forward,
I'll receive God's promised, amazing, reward.
I know it's coming; I feel it in my gut,
If I can just remain calm, while I'm in this rut.
This pain is all temporary, happiness will come.
I'll see God's glory shine upon me again,
When I'm done with *His* life changing plan.

"That which does not kill us makes me stronger."
— Fredrich Nitzche

ABUSER

She thinks about simple arguments, turning into scratches and bruises, as he yells and abuses. She feels like she loses her hope and confidence. She loses herself and becomes what he tells her. She puts her pride on the shelf.

No one will ever love you. No one will ever care. And if you ever try to leave me, when you turn around, I will be there.

So, she sits in the metal prison. She sits in its mental cage. Finally, she gets out with the mentality of a slave. A lot of pain, a lot of rage. A lot of things left unspoken.

Her heart is shattered in pieces. She's confused and broken. She looks for another man thinking this will ease her pain. This guy is different. He doesn't make threats, or leave her with empty promises and bruises. BUT she doesn't know how to act, so she becomes an abuser.

"It is not the bruises on the body that hurt. It is the wounds of the heart and the scars of the mind."
— Aisha Mirza

LONELINESS

This loneliness is beyond repair,
Come on death, take me there.
I never thought I'd pray to die,
Come on, God, hear this cry.
All my hope and faith are gone,
I'm a coward, I'm not that strong.
I feel the punishment of a curse,
I beg, I pray, can it be reversed?
There is so much darkness in my life,
I used to be a mother, and a wife.
Now I'm broken, like shards of glass.
I hope these painful feelings pass.
My mind is a battlefield for good and evil,
I remain confused, body and soul are feeble.
Satan has sent people to toy with my heart.
But God built me kind and loyal from the start.

NO BUSINESS FOR A 10-YEAR-OLD

All my problems began when I was 10 years old. It was 1988. I started growing and smoking marijuana. I was hanging out with the wrong crowd and doing things that a 10-year-old had no business doing.

My parents weren't positive role models. In fact, they introduced me to the drug world. They had me help them grow marijuana commercially. It was a very large-scale operation, producing 100 pounds or more of high-grade marijuana every 6 months. Altogether, well over 200 pounds a year.

I began stealing a pound of weed whenever I wanted. I started selling in middle school, in the 6th grade. I was making thousands of dollars. Everyone wanted to hang out with me because I had lots of money and weed. The older high school kids also wanted to hang out with me, which made me really popular. I threw parties and bought alcohol, LSD and mushrooms. This led to me selling numerous types of drugs. Pretty soon I was a big dealer in Maryland, in the early 1990's, before the 1994 Crime Bill passed.

When this happened, we moved to a different part of Maryland for a few years. After we had been there long enough for me to get know some people who were involved in the drug game, everything started again. I began stealing weed and Acid. I got to know some pretty big players in the game who sold Cocaine. I was only 15 when I started getting high on Cocaine. Then I started smoking Crack…on a regular basis.

One day I got into a fight at school. I beat up the other boy so badly that I go permanently kicked out of school. I never tried to go back to school after that. Instead I found a job doing carpentry work. I was still selling a lot of pot but also started selling Cocaine and Crack. I really kicked it up a notch.

Soon I was drinking and doing drugs for days, even weeks without sleeping. It was the snowball effect, bigger and out of control. At 20 I couldn't see where my life was heading. That's when I started using Heroin and selling it too. I was living with my dad at the time. He kicked me out when he found out what I was doing. So, I moved back in with my mom.

It didn't take long before I met up with old friends and the drug game started again. I met an individual that lived in the inner city and we started going in to buy drugs from the higher ups. I was spinning out of control. Using, then driving to buy more to sell more. We bought Cocaine, Crack and Heroin in the city for cheap and transported it back to our hometown where I could sell it for a lot more money than I paid.

One day I got raided by the Narcotics Police. I was really lucky, they didn't find any drugs, or money because it was all hidden somewhere else. I thought I was untouchable. I didn't lose any money, or drugs that day so I was still in business. I went to court and the charges were dropped due to lack of evidence. I was very lucky. I was making $15,000 a week. The women loved me because of all the drugs I had. I was addicted to the lifestyle of partying, women and money.

I didn't mind that I was getting arrested a few times a year for misdemeanor charges that never really amounted to me doing much time behind bars. One day, a police officer told me that I had been arrested over 40 times.

In 2008, when I was 30 years old, I was just getting released from jail for assault. I was on probation. It did not take long for me to violate probation. I was on the run from the law, again. I didn't want to go back to jail, so my girlfriend and I moved to Florida. I had hoped that moving would bring some positive changes in my life. Wrong! It only took a few months for me to start going in the wrong direction, again. I started the same process. I was back drinking and doing drugs. I ended up losing my apartment because of my addiction. I was homeless and living on the beach. We stayed in homeless camps with strange people and drug addicts from all over the country.

I learned how to pan handle. My girlfriend and I wandered from place to place and set up camp where we could. We were both out panhandling everyday for money to pay for food, alcohol and drugs. Everything we made every day was gone by the next on drugs. This cycle lasted until 2010.

Florida in 2010 was ground zero for Opioids. There were pill mill doctors everywhere. I made up fictitious injuries and got pills. I'd snort some and save some. When I had a big enough supply, I would transport them back to other states and sell them. I quickly got in over my head with the wrong people. Things happened. So, I called a family member and one agreed to get me train ticket back home to Maryland.

During my first few months home things were ok. Then I got into an accident where I injured my hip. I needed to have a hip replacement. I had two different doctors. One prescribed Oxycontin and the other doctor prescribed Roxicodone. Instantly I was back in business selling Opioids. My ex-girlfriend who had stayed in Florida when I returned home, came knocking at my door one night. She asked me if I wanted to get high with her. She had Crystal Meth.

I tried Crystal Meth for the first time with her. I had no idea how bad thing were going to get. I was using faster than I could get it. This is when I found out she knew how to cook it. I helped her and in turn learned how to cook it for myself. I was blind to where my life was headed. Then…

Someone snitched me out to the police. I was arrested for manufacturing Methamphetamine, in West Virginia, in August 2013. I was sentenced to 2-10 years in prison with 5 years of probation upon completing my sentence and a $10,000 fine.

I am currently serving time here at Potomac Highlands Regional Jail in West Virginia. I see the Parole Board in August 2019. I have been attending classes here and have received some certificates and my High School Completion Certificate.

I have a few things to say to people who are wanting to live the lifestyle of selling drugs and living fast without thinking it will end badly. Stop, before it's too late. When you finally get busted, and you will, you lose everything. All the people you thought were your friends forget all about you. When you get locked up, your life will change forever. Stop what you are doing. Change your ways. Ask for help. Before it's too late.

"Nothing is predestined. Obstacles of your past can become the gateways that lead to new beginning."
— Ralph Blum

DEAR KALEY,

This is the hardest letter that I've ever had to write. I need to tell you how sorry I am for not being there for you most of your life. I want you to know that I love you very much. You are my baby girl and I would do anything in the world for you.

I have made so many mistakes in my life. I am paying for each, and every one of them. Right now, I am in jail writing this letter to you. I hope that one day you will read it and forgive me for not being the father you deserved.

I am so sorry, Kaley. I must face this regretful feeling in my heart and soul every day. I think about you, your brothers and your sisters all the time and hope that one day we will all be together again. I dream of us all under one roof. A family having a wonderful time together. I don't know exactly where you are, but I do know you are doing okay. I can't believe that you are already 20 years old! Time really flies by, doesn't it?

I hope that I will be getting out of jail soon. Maybe when I do get released, I can contact you wherever you are? I am almost 2000 miles away from you in this God forsaken place, but I would swim across the ocean to get to you if I had to.

I sit here and wonder what you must look like. What kind of things do you like to do? Do you ever think about me? I remember that you were always happy when I did get to see you on your birthday, or Christmas, or special occasions. Those times and happy memories are few and far between now. Please forgive me for all the times I wasn't there to teach you, help you, or be the father you needed me to be.

I miss you very much. I hope you can one day forgive me for not being there for you. I believe that everything happens for a reason. God is in control of all things. Doing time has given me the opportunity to think about my past, my mistakes, and how I could have done things better. I really messed up, Kaley.

It is my hope that you read this letter and believe deep down that I miss you and love you. I may not have said it often and I know my actions did not show it, but you are the best thing that ever happened to me baby girl; even though things didn't work out between your mother and I. That was and never will be your fault.

I will reach out to you when I get released. I hope and pray that you will talk to me.

Love always your father,
Jacob Gracia

BITTER END

As I walk through the valley of the shadow of death…
That's what happened when I met METH.

My disease controls me. I don't give a shit about anything else.

I am mentally drawn,
My mind keeps screaming until dawn.
Pills, pot, anything I can find,
Please stop this misery in my mind.

The voice screams in my head, "Find something to make this stop!"

It's a torture that is worth taking my life.
I chose this disease over being a mother and a wife.
I no longer have control.
This disease has drained my soul.

This insanity has to stop.
My insanity has reached it's top.
There's nothing left to lose.
This disease doesn't give me a chance to choose.

I've lost everything, including my soul. This disease…it has taken its toll.

Suddenly there's light at the end of the tunnel.
Pour in hope for me with a funnel.
I never thought there was any hope.
I never thought I was going to survive the dope.

God has a different plan for me,
He's cleared my mind so I can see.
No more withdrawal and feeling insane,
Time is slowly healing my brain.

I never knew what it would feel like to feel sane.

I used to doubt there was any hope,
Finally, now, I can cope.
Life today is not that bad.
I don't lay around, hopeless and sad.

I know for once; I'm making Satan mad.

I no longer cry and suffer.
I've become strong-willed and tougher.
This disease will not win.
It's taken me places no one has ever been.

I'm going to fight IT until the bitter end!

 JACOB GRACIA — "CRAZY CLOCK"

BATTLE BORN

INVICTUS

Out of the night that covers me,
Black as the pit from pole to pole,
I thank whatever gods may be
For my unconquerable soul.

In the fell clutch of circumstance
I have not winced nor cried aloud.
Under the bludgeonings of chance
My head is bloody, but unbowed.

Beyond this place of wrath and tears
Looms but the Horror of the shade,
And yet the menace of the years
Finds and shall find me unafraid.

It matters not how strait the gate,
How charged with punishments the scroll,
I am the master of my fate,
I am the captain of my soul.

— *William Earnest Henley*

AFTER YOU GET OUT – THE TRUTH

I believe that people would like to think that getting out of prison is the most exciting, truly happiest day of an incarcerated individuals' life. Well, I am here to tell you that it is, but at the same time it is stressful and terrifying.

In prison your food is cooked for you and brought to you, around the same time each day. Three meals a day. Your laundry is cleaned for you and brought to your pod. Your personal hygiene items: soap, shampoo, toilet paper are also provided. Really, you do not have to worry about the things you will have to buy once you are released.

Now that you are getting ready to be released, it is time to take responsibility for your life and start taking care of yourself…supporting yourself. It would amaze most that the number of people I have met in jail and prison cannot do this. Most inmates have never had or held onto a real job. Most do not have their own home or a car or truck. Really, many of them are lucky to have just one of the things I listed above.

I consider myself fortunate. I grew up working and was raised the "Old Fashioned" way, I guess. My dad taught me that if you wanted something you went out and worked for it, you earned it. So, even though I had been strung out on drugs and broke the law, I always kept my job. I am not sure how I managed to stay employed, but I did.

After getting out this last time, I decided that it was time to change my life around. What I had been doing was not working out for me and I kept ending up back where I started, in jail. This time I moved in with my grandparents, in a new town, away from everything I knew. Personally, it was safer for me to change everything about my life and a new environment offered that to me. I consider myself one of the lucky ones. No one really wants an ex-felon living with them or renting from them, even if they are family.

I struggled at first. I needed a job. I have a good work ethic and have learned many trades over the years: operating equipment, construction, and roofing. However, even being skilled in the trades, I had very little money and no car. Most people turn to their friends for help, but what if your friends are more trouble than the problems that you are dealing with? When I say this I mean, "If I was to have a friend help me with a car, they would want to get high and do dumb shit just to get high again." I cannot do this, so I am on my own.

It is really hard to stay sober when everyone you know, or 90% of them get high on something. What I have learned about myself is that once I start getting high, I cannot stop until I am either back in jail or overdose. When I first walked out the doors of the jail and back to my life it was hard. The

Corona Virus had everything messed up and I did not have to check in or see my Parole Officer for two (2) months.

I had no restrictions. So, I did what most addicts will do. I got high, once. Then it became a roller-coaster ride and I was getting high every day for a month. I was shooting Heroin, Meth, anything I could get my hands on. Everyone around me saw me falling. It was only when I saw and recognized the disappointment in their eyes that something clicked. Their disappointment almost broke me. I realized that my addiction was not only hurting me, it was hurting everyone around me. I knew I had to make a choice. I needed to choose differently this time. At that moment I decided to do something I have never done before. I went and got help, something I have never asked for before. I got in to see a doctor and a counselor. Together they put me on a program.

This is where I am today. I have new friends. I have a new job. I have a new outlook on life and what I really want and that I have a choice on how I want to live my life. Today I am doing good and my job is great. I am about to take a second job, making great money, doing what I love...stonework. My family is impressed with my improvement. I am paying off old debts and bills one week at a time. My Parole is going well, and I have no worries there. I am clean and sober and happy with how things are going in my life.

To make it clear, "Getting out of prison is easy," staying out is where it gets tricky. Changing your life around is fucking hard. You must keep your past in check, or it will consume you and everything you fought for will be for nothing. No one wants to fail or lose. I know now that I am not going back to where I was 2 years ago. To tell you the truth, I would not change my past all that much if I could. My past makes me appreciate all that I have today and what I am doing in my life.

*"Effort and courage are not enough
without purpose and direction"
—JFK*

CONTRIBUTORS BIOS

There were only a few individuals who submitted their own bios for their work. They will know who they are. For those who wished to be anonymous, I respected your anonymity. For all other submissions, I created an author's bio on your behalf. I hope that what I saw in each of you is viewed as a tribute. It was a privilege to be able to work with you and see this compilation come to fruition.

JENNIFER ALFORD #3544848 is respectful and never missed a class. She loved to read and research just about anything about angels. She told me that writing poetry allows her to express her feelings.

JESSICA BUCKINGHAM #3498961 writes, "I am twenty-five years old. I am a high school graduate and have 2 nursing certificates. I have 2 amazing little boys. I like fishing, camping, and being outside."

TORI CORBIN #3540873 said, "I am twenty-seven years old. I was born and raised in Springfield, West Virginia. I have two sisters and the best parents. My children, Ryker Bleu and Bentley Grae are my world. I believe in God, second chances, and miracles. Tori had the desire to change her life. She spent time evaluating her goals and what she truly wants. She was only in class for a short time but made a huge impact on her classmates.

ROBERT GABBERT #3538321 is always up for competition. He brings any team he is a part of together to complete the task and win. He goes outside the box to find a way to come out on top. He is always respectful and helpful in class.

JACOB GRACIA said, "I am the father of four beautiful children: Kaley, Jaylin, Josiah, and Jakob. I was born in San Antonio, Texas. I am currently incarcerated at Potomac Highlands Regional Jail for evading arrest and am serving 2-10 years. I enjoy writing poetry and hope to open a restaurant when I get out so I can bring some Texas flavor to the beautiful state of West Virginia. I strongly believe in this book and hope that it reaches many."

TERRY GRAHAM is as tough as they get on the outside, but speaks of his son with heart. He wants to make sure that his son doesn't fall into the same life he chose or make the same mistakes he has. He always comes to class with a smile and a comment about my shoe choice.

ISAAC HATLEY is intelligent. He sat for all five High School Equivalency Tests on the same day and passed them all on his first try. He found writing poetry challenging at first, but quickly overcame his fear when he realized what he could create.

THOMAS JOHNSON #3604760 always showed up to class with a smile. He was a non-stop talker and constantly asked the tough questions. He challenged the system, is intelligent, and always ready to help. He became one of my first classroom assistants.

VINCENT KELLY-ZITO #3414034 is the only boy in a family of girls. He completed his High School Equivalency while attending class and was excited to be able to wear a cap and gown. He loves to write poetry and letters to his family. Everything he writes comes from the heart.

NIKOLE KEPLINGER always comes to class with an open mind and ready to learn. She is working towards obtaining her High School Completion Certificate. She can't wait to graduate so that she could go to college. She was excited to get released and see her family.

ERIC S. KNIBIEHLY II asked the tough, seemingly, unanswerable questions: why do I do this type of work, do I feel safe, how do I teach all populations? He produced a college level response on *The Count of Monte Cristo* essay. He exhibits complete loyalty to those he calls a friend.

JESSE LONG #3558069 is a team player. He shows true character and loyalty everyday he enters the class. He constantly reaches above and beyond what is asked of him on an assignment. He will go far with his positive attitude.

DAKOTA MACKEY has a brilliant mind and a natural flair for writing. He was only in class for a short time, but reminded me why I enjoy introducing students to writing poetry and creative writing.

JOHN MAUDLIN is soft-spoken, attentive to detail, and polite. He shows up for every class with the goal of learning something new. He is an Army veteran and was deployed four times to serve our country.

ISSAC MAUSALI constantly tries to improve the situation he's in and gain knowledge. He is working diligently toward earning his High School Equivalency. Even when frustrated he is relentless with studying. His drive and work ethic in class is unmatched.

ALLEN E. PARKER JR. #3479874 is one of the most gifted artists I ever met. He has a daughter whom he loves more than life itself. He aspires to go to college and to become a Chemical Dependency Counselor.

CHRISHAWN PERKINS first walked through the door not knowing what a thesaurus was. When he was going to be transferred, he told me that his thesaurus had become like a Bible to him. He loves the meaning and depths that words could express and is excited to share his knowledge with others.

FRANK ROSE #3579683 came to class and obtained his High School Equivalency in a very short time. He is quiet, diligent, and goes the extra mile to finish his work. He is an amazing artist.

MISTY SELLERS said, "I am a forty-two-year-old widow with two amazing daughters: Jordan and Jaime (Rudy) Sellers. I have a family that I love very much. I love dirt bike riding, camping, and swimming. I love to laugh and have a good time all the time." She has an infectious laugh that makes everyone around her smile.

ADAM SHIPWAY is one of the students that I had in class the longest. He worked very hard to be able to wear a cap and gown when he passed his High School Equivalency Exam. He is humble, compassionate, and inquisitive.

MICHEAL SMITH-BARROW came to class every day and is working toward earning his High School Equivalency. He is a gifted and private writer. I hope he realizes his talent. He is aware of how he ended up in his situation, but is striving to achieve something better.

ANGELA WHITE #3594957 is quick to make others laugh. She can't wait to get released and see her family. She wants to have the ability to go back to school and start a career. She loves her children more than anything.

ALEXUS WOODS is sharp as a tack. She loves music and her moral compass is intact. She outwardly takes blame for where she is and expresses her desire to change so that she can go home and start a better life.

9 798673 301500